The Universe Talks

Unlocking the Language of Vibration and Manifesting Your Desired Reality

Jamie Morgan

Contents

Introduction

The universe is a mirror, reflecting the essence of your consciousness in every experience, thought, and emotion you encounter. Your reality is not a coincidence but a direct manifestation of the energy you emit and the focus you give to the various aspects of your life. Just as celestial bodies orbit the sun, your perceptions and feelings revolve around the gravitational center of your awareness, shaping your world profoundly.

Recognizing the power of your attention is key to creating the life you desire. Where you invest your energy and focus is what the universe reflects back to you. Every thought and action is a choice that contributes to the overall picture of your reality. The challenge is that we often navigate this process unconsciously, unaware of our incredible influence over our lives.

To truly harness the power of your attention and manifest your deepest desires, you must understand the language of energy. The universe communicates through vibrations and frequencies that resonate with your core being. Your thoughts, emotions, and actions carry a distinct energetic signature that attracts similar experiences into your life.

By learning to consciously direct your attention toward the positive and uplifting, you can shift your vibrational frequency and align yourself with the abundance and joy the universe offers. This empowers you to become a master of your reality and a co-creator with the divine.

However, this journey requires deep introspection, confronting limiting beliefs, and committing to personal growth. Throughout this book, we will explore practical techniques for:

1. Cultivating mindfulness and awareness of your thoughts and emotions

2. Directing your attention to manifest your goals and desires

3. Interpreting the messages and guidance the universe provides

4. Reframing challenges as opportunities for growth and learning

5. Aligning your energy with the flow of cosmic intelligence

By implementing these strategies, you'll discover that the obstacles you face are not random but rather stepping stones to realizing your greatest potential. Embracing these experiences with openness and curiosity will propel you closer to the life you dream of.

As you embark on this transformative journey, remember that every insight is a catalyst for change, and every step is a testament to your incredible capacity for growth. Welcome to the world of consciousness, energy, and the infinite possibilities available to you. May this book guide you to align with the heartbeat of the universe and create a reality that reflects your deepest truth.

Chapter One

The Power of
Attention

Your attention is a vote for amplification, a cosmic ballot cast with every thought, feeling, and action you choose to engage with. The universe, in its infinite wisdom, is constantly listening, registering every vibration you emit and responding in kind. When you focus on something, whether positive or negative, you are sending a clear message to the universe that says, "More of this, please."

This is the fundamental principle behind the art of selective engagement. By consciously choosing where to place your attention, you are actively participating in the creation of your reality. Every moment presents an opportunity to either reinforce the patterns and experiences you desire or to perpetuate those that no longer serve you.

Consider the thoughts that run through your mind on a daily basis. Are they dominated by worry, fear, and self-doubt, or are they filled with gratitude, joy, and self-love? The quality of your thoughts is a direct reflection of the quality of your life, for the universe is a faithful mirror, reflecting back to you the energy you put out.

The same principle applies to your emotions and actions. When you allow yourself to be consumed by anger, resentment, or frustration, you are inviting more of those low-vibrational experiences into your life. On the other hand, when you choose to cultivate feelings of love, compassion, and forgiveness, you are aligning yourself with the higher frequencies of the universe, attracting more positive experiences and opportunities.

Mastering the art of selective engagement requires a deep understanding of the power of your attention and a willingness to take responsibility for the energy you bring to each moment. It means becoming mindful of your thoughts, emotions, and actions, and consciously redirecting your focus toward that which you wish to manifest in your life.

This is not always easy, especially in the face of life's challenges and obstacles. It can be tempting to get caught up in the drama and negativity of a situation, to allow yourself to be swept away by the currents of fear and doubt. But remember, you always have a choice. You can choose to focus on the problem, or you can choose to focus on the solution. You can choose to dwell on what's not working, or you can choose to appreciate what is.

By consistently choosing to place your attention on the positive aspects of your life, on the things you are grateful for, and on the experiences you wish to create, you are sending a powerful message to the universe. You are saying, "This is what I want more of. This is what I am ready to receive."

As you begin to master the art of selective engagement, you will notice a shift in your reality. Synchronicities and opportunities will start to appear, as if by magic. You will find yourself attracted to people and situations that align with your highest vision for your life. And you will begin to experience a sense of ease and flow, as you release resistance and allow the universe to work on your behalf.

Withholding attention to communicate disinterest is the flip side of the coin, an equally potent tool in the art of selective engagement. Just as focusing your attention on something amplifies its presence in your life, withdrawing your attention sends a clear signal to the universe that you are no longer interested in experiencing that particular energy or situation.

This is a critical skill to cultivate, especially in a world that is constantly vying for your attention, bombarding you with messages, notifications, and demands from all directions. It can be easy to get caught up in the noise, to allow your attention to be hijacked by the latest crisis or controversy, even if it has nothing to do with your own life or goals.

But when you learn to consciously withhold your attention from the things that don't serve you, you are reclaiming your power and your peace. You are sending a message to the universe that says, "I am not available for this. I choose not to engage with this energy."

This doesn't mean that you are ignoring your problems or challenges, or that you are in denial about the difficulties you may be facing. Rather, it means that you are choosing to focus your attention on the solutions, on the actions you can take to move forward, rather than getting bogged down in the drama and negativity of the situation.

For example, let's say you are in a toxic relationship or work environment, where you constantly feel drained, unappreciated, or even abused. It can be tempting to dwell on the injustice of the situation, to get caught up in the stories of victimhood and powerlessness. But when you consciously choose to withhold your attention from the negativity, when you refuse to engage with the energy of the situation, you are taking back your power.

Instead of focusing on what's not working, you can choose to focus on what you want to create. You can start to envision a new reality for yourself, one where you are surrounded by love, respect, and appreciation. You can take practical steps to extricate yourself from the toxic situation, whether that means setting boundaries, seeking support, or even walking away altogether.

The key is to remember that your attention is a form of energy, and that energy flows where your attention goes. When you withhold your attention from something, you are essentially starving it of the energy it needs to thrive. Over time, that thing will start to wither and fade from your experience, making room for new, more positive experiences to take its place.

Of course, this is not always a quick or easy process. It takes practice and persistence to retrain your mind and redirect your attention, especially if you have been in a pattern of focusing on the negative for a long time. But with commitment and consistency, you can begin to shift your reality, one choice at a time.

So start small. Notice where your attention is going throughout the day, and consciously choose to withdraw it from the things that don't align with your highest vision for your life. Focus instead on the things that bring you joy, that inspire you, that make you feel alive and empowered.

Remember, you are the master of your attention, and therefore the master of your reality. Choose wisely, and watch as your world begins to reflect the beauty and abundance of your innermost desires.

Co-creating your reality through selective engagement is the ultimate expression of your power as a conscious being in an interconnected universe. It is the recognition that your attention is not just a passive observer of your life, but an active participant in shaping your experiences, relationships, and circumstances.

When you begin to view your attention as a creative force, you start to realize that every moment is an opportunity to collaborate with the universe in bringing your deepest desires and aspirations to life. You are not just a recipient of your reality, but a co-creator, working in partnership with the cosmic intelligence that underlies all things.

This is a profound shift in perspective, one that requires a deep level of trust and surrender. It means letting go of the need to control every outcome, and instead aligning yourself with the flow of the universe, trusting that your highest good is always being served, even when things don't unfold as you had planned.

It also means taking responsibility for your own energy and vibration, recognizing that the quality of your attention directly influences the quality of your life. When you focus on lack, scarcity, and limitation, you are sending a message to the universe that this is what you expect to experience. But when you focus on abundance, joy, and possibilities, you are opening yourself up to receive the very best that life has to offer.

One powerful way to co-create your reality through selective engagement is to practice the art of visualization. This involves using your imagination to create a vivid, sensory-rich experience of the reality you wish to manifest, as if it were already happening in the present moment.

For example, if you want to attract a loving, harmonious relationship into your life, you might spend a few minutes each day visualizing yourself in the presence of your ideal partner. See yourself laughing together, holding hands, feeling the warmth and connection between you. Allow yourself to fully embody the feelings of love, joy, and fulfillment that this relationship brings you.

As you engage in this practice consistently, you are sending a clear signal to the universe that this is the reality you are ready to experience. You are aligning your energy with the vibration of love and partnership, and in doing so, you are magnetizing those experiences into your life.

The same principle applies to any area of your life that you wish to transform, whether it's your health, your career, your finances, or your personal growth. By selectively engaging your attention on the outcomes you desire, and allowing yourself to fully feel the positive emotions associated with those outcomes, you are co-creating your reality in partnership with the universe.

Of course, this doesn't mean that you can simply sit back and wait for your desires to manifest without taking any action. Co-creation is a dance between your intentions and your actions, between your faith and your follow-through. It requires a willingness to show up fully in each moment, to take inspired action when guided, and to trust in the unfolding of your journey.

But when you master the art of selective engagement, when you learn to harness the power of your attention and align it with the wisdom of the universe, you open yourself up to a world of infinite possibilities. You become a true co-creator, a sovereign being who is actively shaping your reality in every moment.

So start today. Choose one area of your life that you wish to transform, and begin to engage your attention on the outcomes you desire. Allow yourself to feel the positive emotions associated with those outcomes, and trust that the universe is conspiring in your favor, bringing you the people, opportunities, and resources you need to make your dreams a reality.

Remember, you are a powerful creator, a divine being with the ability to shape your world through the focus of your attention. Embrace this truth, and watch as your life unfolds in miraculous and beautiful ways.

Chapter Two

Navigating the Unconscious Process

Becoming conscious of your attention investment is the first step in mastering the art of selective engagement and harnessing the power of your focus to create the reality you desire. Much of our attention is invested unconsciously, driven by habits, patterns, and conditioning that we have absorbed throughout our lives. This unconscious investment of attention can often lead us to perpetuate experiences and situations that no longer serve our highest good, keeping us stuck in cycles of negativity, lack, and limitation.

To break free from these unconscious patterns, we must first bring them into the light of our awareness. This requires a willingness to turn our attention inward, to observe our thoughts, emotions, and reactions with curiosity and non-judgment. By becoming conscious of where our attention is habitually invested, we can begin to recognize the ways in which we may be unconsciously contributing to our own suffering and blocking the flow of abundance and joy in our lives.

One powerful tool for becoming conscious of your attention investment is the practice of mindfulness. Mindfulness is the simple act of bringing your awareness to the present moment, observing your inner experience without getting caught up in the stories or judgments that your mind creates. By cultivating mindfulness, you can begin to notice the subtle ways in which your attention is being pulled in different directions, and the impact that this has on your emotional state and overall well-being.

For example, you might notice that when you invest your attention in worrying about the future, you experience feelings of anxiety and stress. Or, when you dwell on past hurts or resentments, you feel a sense of heaviness and contraction in your body. These observations can be valuable clues, pointing you towards the areas of your life where your attention is being unconsciously invested in ways that are not serving you.

As you become more conscious of your attention investment, you can begin to make more intentional choices about where to direct your focus. This might involve setting aside time each day for practices that help you to cultivate positive, life-affirming states of mind, such as gratitude, compassion, and joy. It might also involve learning to recognize and disengage from negative thought patterns or limiting beliefs that are draining your energy and holding you back from your full potential.

Another important aspect of becoming conscious of your attention investment is learning to recognize the external influences that may be shaping your focus in unconscious ways. In today's world, we are constantly bombarded with media messages, social pressures, and cultural conditioning that can lead us to invest our attention in pursuits that are ultimately unfulfilling or even harmful. By becoming more aware of these external influences, we can begin to make more discerning choices about the information and experiences we allow into our consciousness.

Ultimately, becoming conscious of your attention investment is a ongoing process of self-discovery and self-mastery. It requires a commitment to turning inward, to embracing the full spectrum of your human experience with openness and curiosity. As you develop a deeper understanding of the ways in which your attention shapes your reality, you can begin to wield this power with greater intention and purpose, co-creating a life that is truly aligned with your deepest values and aspirations.

The impact of unconscious navigation on your experiences is a crucial aspect of understanding the power of attention and the art of selective engagement. When we navigate through life unconsciously, without being fully aware of the thoughts, beliefs, and patterns that are shaping our perception and behavior, we often find ourselves feeling stuck, unfulfilled, or even powerless in the face of our circumstances.

At the core of this unconscious navigation is a fundamental misunderstanding about the nature of reality and our role in co-creating our experiences. When we operate from a place of unconsciousness, we tend to see ourselves as passive recipients of life's events, rather than active participants in shaping our own destinies. We may feel like victims of our circumstances, blaming external factors for our problems and challenges, rather than recognizing the ways in which our own attention and energy are contributing to these experiences.

One of the most significant impacts of unconscious navigation is that it often leads us to repeat the same patterns and experiences over and over again, even when they are not serving our highest good. This is because our unconscious mind is primarily driven by habit and conditioning, and will often seek out experiences that feel familiar or comfortable, even if they are ultimately limiting or harmful.

For example, if we have grown up with a belief that we are not worthy of love and respect, we may unconsciously invest our attention in relationships or situations that reinforce this belief, attracting partners who treat us poorly or settling for less than we deserve. Similarly, if we have internalized a sense of scarcity or lack, we may unconsciously focus our attention on the ways in which we feel deprived or disadvantaged, rather than cultivating an attitude of gratitude and abundance.

Over time, these unconscious patterns of attention can become deeply ingrained, shaping our perceptions, beliefs, and behaviors in ways that limit our potential and keep us stuck in cycles of negativity and suffering. We may find ourselves feeling chronically anxious, depressed, or unfulfilled, without fully understanding why.

The good news is that by becoming more conscious of our attention and the ways in which it is shaping our experiences, we can begin to break free from these unconscious patterns and create a new reality for ourselves. This requires a willingness to turn inward, to observe our thoughts and emotions with curiosity and non-judgment, and to take responsibility for the energy we are bringing to each moment.

One powerful tool for navigating the unconscious process is the practice of self-inquiry. This involves asking ourselves honest questions about the beliefs, assumptions, and patterns that are driving our behavior and shaping our experiences. For example, we might ask ourselves:

- What thoughts or beliefs do I have about myself and my abilities?

- What patterns do I notice in my relationships or interactions with others?

- What emotions or physical sensations arise when I think about certain aspects of my life?

- What stories or narratives do I tell myself about my past, present, or future?

By bringing these unconscious patterns into the light of our awareness, we can begin to challenge and transform them, replacing limiting beliefs with more empowering ones, and investing our attention in experiences that truly nourish and inspire us.

Another key aspect of navigating the unconscious process is developing a greater sense of presence and mindfulness in our daily lives. By learning to anchor our attention in the present moment, rather than getting caught up in regrets about the past or worries about the future, we can begin to disengage from unconscious patterns of thought and emotion and connect with a deeper sense of clarity and purpose.

Techniques for conscious attention management are essential tools for anyone seeking to master the art of selective engagement and harness the power of their focus to create a more fulfilling and purposeful life. By developing a repertoire of practices and strategies for managing our attention, we can begin to navigate the complexities of our inner and outer worlds with greater skill, resilience, and adaptability.

One foundational technique for conscious attention management is the practice of mindfulness meditation. Mindfulness is the simple act of bringing our attention to the present moment, observing our thoughts, emotions, and sensations without judgment or resistance. By cultivating a regular practice of mindfulness, we can begin to develop a greater sense of clarity, calm, and centeredness, even in the midst of life's challenges and distractions.

To practice mindfulness meditation, find a quiet and comfortable place where you can sit or lie down without interruption. Close your eyes and begin by taking a few deep, slow breaths, allowing your body to settle and relax. Then, gently bring your attention to your breath, noticing the sensations of the air moving in and out of your nostrils or the rise and fall of your chest. Whenever you notice your mind wandering, simply acknowledge the distraction without judgment and gently guide your attention back to your breath.

With regular practice, mindfulness meditation can help us to develop a greater sense of awareness and control over our attention, allowing us to disengage from unhelpful patterns of thought and emotion and cultivate a more positive and purposeful state of mind.

Another powerful technique for conscious attention management is the practice of reframing. Reframing involves consciously choosing to shift our perspective on a particular situation or experience, looking for the opportunities and lessons that may be hidden within even the most challenging circumstances.

For example, if we find ourselves feeling overwhelmed or frustrated by a difficult project at work, we might choose to reframe the situation as an opportunity to develop new skills, build resilience, or demonstrate our value to the organization. By consciously shifting our attention to the potential benefits and growth opportunities within the challenge, we can begin to transform our experience and cultivate a more positive and empowered state of mind.

Other techniques for conscious attention management might include:

- Practicing gratitude: Consciously focusing our attention on the things we are grateful for, no matter how small, can help to shift our perspective and cultivate a more positive and abundant mindset.

- Setting intentions: Taking a few moments each day to consciously set intentions for how we want to show up and what we want to create can help to align our attention and energy with our deepest values and aspirations.

- Cultivating self-compassion: Learning to treat ourselves with kindness, understanding, and forgiveness, even in the face of our own mistakes and imperfections, can help to reduce stress and anxiety and cultivate a more resilient and adaptable mindset.

- Engaging in flow activities: Pursuits that fully engage our attention and challenge us to stretch beyond our current abilities, such as creative hobbies, sports, or intellectual pursuits, can help to cultivate a sense of flow and fulfillment and strengthen our ability to focus and manage our attention.

Ultimately, the key to conscious attention management is to approach it as an ongoing practice, rather than a one-time fix. By consistently engaging in techniques and strategies that help us to cultivate greater awareness, intentionality, and resilience, we can begin to transform our relationship with our own minds and tap into the limitless potential that lies within us.

As we deepen our mastery of conscious attention management, we may find that we are able to navigate even the most challenging and complex situations with greater ease, grace, and effectiveness. We may discover a newfound sense of clarity, purpose, and empowerment, as we learn to co-create our reality in alignment with our deepest values and aspirations.

So, whether you are just beginning your journey of self-discovery and personal growth, or are a seasoned practitioner looking to deepen your skills and insights, the practice of conscious attention management offers a powerful pathway to greater self-awareness, resilience, and fulfillment. By committing to this ongoing practice, you can begin to unlock the full potential of your mind and spirit, and create a life of true abundance, joy, and purpose.

Chapter Three

The Language of the Present Moment

The universe's recognition of the "now" as reality is a fundamental principle that underlies the practice of conscious attention management and the art of co-creating one's experience. In the ever-unfolding tapestry of existence, the present moment is the only point of true power and possibility, the nexus from which all thoughts, actions, and manifestations arise.

From the perspective of the universe, past and future are merely mental constructs, projections of the mind that have no inherent reality. The past is a collection of memories and experiences that have already transpired, while the future is a realm of potentiality and imagination, shaped by our hopes, fears, and expectations. While these mental constructs can certainly influence our present experience, they do not hold the same creative power as the here and now.

In the present moment, we have the ability to consciously choose our focus, our actions, and our energetic state. We can attune ourselves to the subtle currents of inspiration and intuition that flow through the universe, aligning our intentions and behaviors with the unfolding of our highest path. By anchoring our attention in the now, we open ourselves to the infinite possibilities that exist within each passing moment, unrestricted by the limiting beliefs and patterns of the past or the anxieties and projections of the future.

The language of the present moment is one of immediacy, spontaneity, and responsiveness. It is a language that values presence, awareness, and adaptability over rigid planning or rumination. When we learn to speak this language fluently, we become more attuned to the natural rhythms and cycles of life, more receptive to the opportunities and synchronicities that arise in our path.

One of the key challenges in mastering the language of the present moment is overcoming the mind's tendency to drift into past or future-oriented thought patterns. The human mind is a complex and powerful tool, capable of incredible feats of imagination, problem-solving, and creativity. However, when left unchecked, it can also become a source of distraction, anxiety, and self-limitation, pulling us out of the present moment and into a world of mental chatter and projection.

To cultivate a deeper fluency in the language of the now, it is essential to develop practices that help to anchor our attention in the present moment. Mindfulness meditation, as explored in the previous chapter, is one such practice that can be incredibly effective in training the mind to rest more fully in the here and now. By regularly bringing our attention back to the breath, the body, or the sensory details of our immediate experience, we strengthen our ability to disengage from distracting thoughts and tune into the richness and vividness of the unfolding moment.

Another powerful practice for aligning with the language of the now is to cultivate a sense of curiosity and openness towards each moment as it arises. Rather than approaching life with a fixed agenda or a predetermined set of expectations, we can learn to meet each moment with a sense of wonder and receptivity, trusting in the inherent wisdom and rightness of the universe's unfolding.

This practice of curious, open attention can be applied to even the most mundane or challenging aspects of our lives. When we encounter difficulties or obstacles, rather than getting lost in stories of victimhood or blame, we can choose to approach the situation with a sense of interest and exploration, asking ourselves: "What is this moment inviting me to learn or discover? How can I respond with presence and creativity to the challenges that arise?"

By cultivating this sense of curiosity and presence, we begin to shift our relationship with the present moment, seeing it not as something to be resisted or controlled, but as a dynamic and evolving field of potential that we can learn to navigate with skill and grace. We become more responsive to the subtle cues and invitations that arise within our experience, more attuned to the natural flow and unfolding of our lives.

Ultimately, the language of the present moment is a language of trust, surrender, and co-creation. It requires a willingness to let go of our attachments to specific outcomes or timelines, and to instead align ourselves with the greater intelligence and creativity of the universe. By learning to rest more fully in the now, we open ourselves to a world of limitless possibility and potential, co-creating our reality in partnership with the ever-unfolding mystery of existence.

Thinking and speaking in the present tense is a powerful practice that can help us to more fully embody the language of the now and align our consciousness with the generative power of the present moment. When we focus our thoughts and words on the current experience, rather than getting caught up in narratives about the past or projections about the future, we tap into a greater sense of clarity, authenticity, and creative potential.

One of the key benefits of thinking and speaking in the present tense is that it helps to anchor our attention in the immediacy of the unfolding moment. By directing our mental and verbal energy towards what is happening right here and now, we cultivate a greater sense of presence and attunement to the subtle nuances and opportunities that arise within our experience. We become more responsive to the needs and invitations of the moment, rather than getting lost in abstractions or distractions.

This practice of present-tense thinking and speaking is particularly valuable when it comes to setting intentions and affirming our desires. Often, when we think or speak about our goals and aspirations, we frame them in terms of the future, saying things like "I will be successful" or "I hope to find love." While there is certainly value in having a clear vision for the future, this future-oriented language can sometimes reinforce a sense of separation or lack, implying that the things we desire are not available to us in the present moment.

By contrast, when we shift our language to the present tense, affirming statements like "I am successful" or "I am loved," we tap into a greater sense of ownership and embodiment of these qualities. We begin to align our energy and awareness with the truth of our being, recognizing that the things we seek are not distant or unattainable, but are in fact inherent aspects of our nature that we can access and express in the here and now.

This shift in language and perspective can be particularly transformative when it comes to working with limiting beliefs or self-doubt. Often, these negative thought patterns are rooted in past experiences or future fears, keeping us trapped in a cycle of self-limitation and anxiety. By consciously choosing to reframe these thoughts in the present tense, focusing on what is true and available to us in the current moment, we begin to loosen the grip of these limiting beliefs and open ourselves to new possibilities and perspectives.

For example, instead of thinking "I have always been bad at public speaking," we can choose to affirm "I am becoming more confident and expressive in my communication." Instead of worrying "I will never find a fulfilling career," we can focus on "I am open to discovering new opportunities and aligning my work with my passions." By shifting our language to the present tense, we begin to retrain our minds to look for evidence of our desired qualities and experiences in the here and now, rather than getting lost in stories of lack or limitation.

Of course, the practice of present-tense thinking and speaking is not about denying or suppressing difficult emotions or experiences. It is important to acknowledge and honor the full range of our human experience, including the challenges and struggles that inevitably arise. However, by choosing to meet these experiences with a sense of presence and compassion, rather than getting lost in stories of victimhood or blame, we can begin to transform our relationship to them and find greater freedom and empowerment in the present moment.

Ultimately, the practice of thinking and speaking in the present tense is about aligning our consciousness with the creative power and potential of the now. By focusing our attention and intention on what is true and available to us in the current moment, we begin to tap into a greater sense of clarity, authenticity, and possibility. We become more responsive to the invitations and opportunities that arise within our experience, more attuned to the wisdom and intelligence of the universe as it unfolds through us.

As we deepen our mastery of this practice, we may find that our relationship to time itself begins to shift and expand. Rather than feeling trapped in a linear progression of past, present, and future, we begin to experience time as a fluid and malleable field of possibility, shaped by the quality of our attention and intention in each passing moment. We recognize that the present moment is not just a fleeting instant, but a gateway to the infinite potential and creativity of the universe, available to us in every breath and every choice.

By embracing the power and potential of the present tense, we open ourselves to a new way of being and relating to the world around us.

We become more grounded, more authentic, and more attuned to the magic and mystery of the unfolding journey. And as we learn to think and speak from this place of presence and possibility, we begin to co-create a reality that is more aligned with our deepest truths and most cherished aspirations.

Embodying your desires in the present moment is a transformative practice that allows you to tap into the creative power of the universe and manifest your deepest aspirations with greater ease and flow. Rather than seeing your desires as distant goals to be strived for in the future, this practice invites you to align your energy and awareness with the essence of what you seek, right here and now.

At its core, embodying your desires is about shifting your vibrational frequency to match the qualities and experiences you wish to attract into your life. It is a recognition that everything in the universe is made up of energy, and that like attracts like. When you focus your attention and intention on the feelings and sensations associated with your desires, you begin to attune yourself to the frequency of those experiences, drawing them towards you with greater magnetism and grace.

One of the key aspects of embodying your desires is to engage all of your senses in the process. Rather than simply thinking about what you want, take time to visualize it in vivid detail, as if it were already a reality in your present moment experience. See yourself living and expressing the qualities and experiences you desire, and allow yourself to fully feel the emotions and sensations that arise in your body as you do so.

For example, if one of your deepest desires is to experience more love and connection in your life, take a moment to close your eyes and imagine yourself surrounded by loving, supportive relationships. Visualize the faces of the people in your life who cherish and appreciate you, and feel the warmth and joy that arises in your heart as you do so. Notice the sensations of openness, expansiveness, and gratitude that flow through your body, and allow yourself to fully embody the energy of love and connection in this moment.

As you practice embodying your desires in this way, you may find that your perception of reality begins to shift and expand. Rather than seeing the world as a fixed and limited place, you begin to recognize the infinite possibilities and potentials that exist within each moment. You start to notice synchronicities and opportunities that align with your deepest aspirations, and you feel a greater sense of trust and flow in the unfolding of your life.

Another key aspect of embodying your desires is to cultivate a sense of gratitude and appreciation for the blessings and abundance that are already present in your life. Often, when we are focused on the things we lack or the goals we have yet to achieve, we overlook the incredible gifts and opportunities that surround us in each moment. By taking time to acknowledge and appreciate the beauty, love, and abundance that already exist in your reality, you begin to shift your vibrational frequency to one of receptivity and grace, opening yourself to even greater blessings and miracles.

This practice of gratitude and appreciation can be as simple as taking a few moments each day to reflect on the things you are thankful for, no matter how small or seemingly insignificant. It can involve expressing your appreciation to the people in your life who support and inspire you, or taking time to savor the simple joys and pleasures of the present moment - the warmth of the sun on your skin, the taste of a delicious meal, the laughter of a loved one.

As you cultivate this sense of gratitude and appreciation, you may find that your relationship to your desires begins to shift and evolve. Rather than seeing them as something to be grasped or strived for, you begin to recognize that they are already a part of your being, waiting to be expressed and manifested in the world. You start to trust in the universe's ability to bring you what you need, in the perfect time and way, and you release your attachment to specific outcomes or timelines.

Ultimately, the practice of embodying your desires in the present moment is about aligning yourself with the creative power and intelligence of the universe, and allowing that power to flow through you in every moment. It is a recognition that you are not separate from the things you seek, but are in fact a unique and essential expression of the universal energy of creation.

By focusing your attention and intention on the qualities and experiences you wish to manifest, and cultivating a sense of gratitude and appreciation for the blessings that are already present in your life, you begin to tap into a profound sense of joy, freedom, and possibility. You become a powerful co-creator of your reality, shaping your world from a place of presence, authenticity, and love.

As you deepen your practice of embodying your desires, you may find that your life begins to unfold in miraculous and unexpected ways. Doors open where there once seemed to be only walls, and opportunities arise that align perfectly with your deepest passions and purposes. You begin to live from a place of true abundance and grace, recognizing that everything you need is already within you, waiting to be expressed and shared with the world.

Chapter Four

Expanding Your Consciousness

L ife as a dynamic and interactive game is a powerful metaphor for understanding the nature of reality and our role in co-creating our experiences. When we begin to view existence as a vast, ever-evolving playground of possibilities, we open ourselves to a new level of awareness and potential. This shift in perspective invites us to step into our full power as conscious agents, actively participating in the unfolding of our own destinies.

In the game of life, we are not mere spectators or passive recipients of circumstance, but rather dynamic players, each with our own unique set of skills, challenges, and opportunities. Every moment presents a new chance to make a move, to choose a direction, and to explore the infinite possibilities that lie before us. The key to mastering this game lies in expanding our consciousness, broadening our awareness of the multifaceted dimensions of reality.

One of the foundational aspects of expanding consciousness is developing a keen understanding of the rules and principles that govern the game of life. Just as any skilled player must learn the mechanics and strategies of their chosen game, we too must cultivate a deep knowledge of the universal laws and patterns that shape our experiences. This includes concepts such as the law of attraction, the power of intention, and the dynamics of energy and vibration.

By studying and integrating these principles into our lives, we begin to develop a more sophisticated understanding of how our thoughts, beliefs, and actions influence the unfolding of our reality. We learn to recognize the subtle feedback loops and synchronicities that reflect our internal state and provide clues to the next steps on our path. We become more attuned to the language of the universe, the whispers of intuition and inspiration that guide us towards our highest potential.

Another key aspect of expanding consciousness is cultivating a practice of deep self-reflection and introspection. In the game of life, our greatest opponent is often our own limiting beliefs, fears, and patterns of self-sabotage. By turning our attention inward and exploring the depths of our own psyche, we begin to uncover the hidden scripts and narratives that shape our perceptions and experiences.

This process of self-discovery can be challenging, as it requires us to confront aspects of ourselves that we may have long denied or suppressed. However, by bringing these shadow elements into the light of awareness, we can begin to heal, integrate, and transform them. We learn to recognise the gifts and lessons hidden within our wounds, and to use our challenges as fuel for our growth and evolution.

One powerful tool for expanding consciousness through self-reflection is the practice of journaling. By regularly writing down our thoughts, feelings, and experiences, we create a sacred space for honest self-expression and exploration. We can use our journal as a mirror, reflecting back to us the patterns and themes that emerge in our lives, and helping us to gain clarity and insight into our own inner workings.

Another valuable technique for self-discovery is the use of personality typologies or archetypal frameworks, such as the Enneagram or the Myers-Briggs Type Indicator. These systems provide a structured way of understanding the different facets of human personality, and can help us to identify our own unique strengths, challenges, and growth edges. By exploring these frameworks with curiosity and openness, we can gain a deeper appreciation for the diversity of human experience and learn to navigate our relationships with greater skill and compassion.

As we deepen our self-awareness and expand our consciousness, we may also find it helpful to seek out the guidance and support of mentors, teachers, or spiritual communities. In the game of life, we are not meant to go it alone, but rather to learn from and collaborate with others who share our values and aspirations. By surrounding ourselves with individuals who challenge and inspire us, we can accelerate our growth and expand our perspective in ways that may not be possible on our own.

Ultimately, the process of expanding consciousness is a journey of remembering our true nature as infinite, creative beings. It is a path of awakening to the vast potential that lies within us, and learning to align ourselves with the evolutionary impulse of the universe. As we grow in awareness and understanding, we begin to recognize that the game of life is not a competition or a struggle, but rather a grand adventure, an opportunity to explore the boundless possibilities of existence.

By embracing this perspective, we can approach the challenges and obstacles that arise with a sense of curiosity, resilience, and even joy. We learn to see every moment as a chance to learn, to grow, and to express our unique gifts and talents in service of something greater than ourselves. We become active co-creators of our reality, shaping our experiences with intention and grace.

As we expand our consciousness and deepen our engagement with the game of life, we may find that our priorities and values begin to shift. We may feel called to pursue a greater sense of purpose and meaning, to contribute to the healing and transformation of our world in whatever way feels authentic and aligned for us. We may discover new depths of compassion, wisdom, and creativity within ourselves, and learn to channel these qualities into our relationships, our work, and our communities.

Ultimately, the journey of expanding consciousness is a lifelong process, an ever-unfolding adventure of discovery and transformation. It requires patience, persistence, and a willingness to embrace the unknown, to step beyond the comfort of our familiar patterns and beliefs. Yet, as we navigate this path with courage and curiosity, we open ourselves to a world of infinite possibility, a reality that is more vibrant, connected, and alive than we could have ever imagined.

By committing ourselves to the ongoing practice of expanding our consciousness, we become active participants in the evolution of our species and the unfolding of a new paradigm on our planet. We recognise that the game of life is not a solo endeavour, but rather a collective journey, a dance of co-creation with the greater intelligence and creativity of the universe. As we awaken to our true nature and potential, we become beacons of light and inspiration for others, catalysing a ripple effect of transformation that extends far beyond our individual lives.

So, let us embrace the adventure of expanding our consciousness with open hearts and minds. Let us approach the game of life with a sense of wonder, gratitude, and possibility, knowing that every moment is an opportunity to learn, to grow, and to make a difference in the world. As we navigate the ups and downs of this journey, let us remember that we are never alone, but always held in the loving embrace of a universe that is conspiring in our favour, guiding us towards our highest truth and potential. May we have the courage and the grace to answer this call, and to play our unique role in the grand unfolding of existence.

Broadening your awareness of inner self, thought patterns, and the universe is a fundamental aspect of expanding consciousness and deepening your engagement with the game of life. As you cultivate a more intimate understanding of your own internal landscape, you begin to recognize the ways in which your thoughts, beliefs, and emotions shape your experience of reality. Simultaneously, as you attune yourself to the vast intelligence and complexity of the universe, you open yourself to new levels of insight, inspiration, and guidance.

One powerful tool for broadening self-awareness is the practice of mindfulness. By learning to observe your thoughts and emotions with a sense of detachment and curiosity, you begin to liberate yourself from the reactive patterns and conditioning that often drive your behavior. You learn to recognize the transient nature of mental phenomena, and to cultivate a sense of equanimity and resilience in the face of life's challenges.

To cultivate mindfulness, you might explore practices such as body scanning, where you systematically bring your attention to different regions of your physical being, noticing any sensations, tensions, or areas of ease. You might also experiment with labeling your thoughts and emotions as they arise, silently acknowledging them without judgment or engagement. Over time, these practices can help you to develop a more spacious and compassionate relationship with your inner world, and to respond to life's situations with greater clarity and intention.

Another valuable avenue for broadening self-awareness is the exploration of your core values and beliefs. By taking the time to reflect on what truly matters to you, and to examine the underlying assumptions and narratives that shape your worldview, you can begin to align your life with a deeper sense of purpose and authenticity. You might engage in exercises such as values clarification, where you identify and prioritize the principles and qualities that are most essential to your well-being and fulfilment.

As you deepen your self-awareness, you may also find it fruitful to explore the realm of shadow work. This involves courageously confronting the aspects of yourself that you tend to deny, suppress, or project onto others. By bringing these hidden dimensions of your psyche into the light of consciousness, you can begin to integrate and heal them, liberating vast reserves of energy and potential that were previously trapped in patterns of resistance and fear.

One tool for shadow work is the practice of active imagination, where you engage in a conscious dialogue with different aspects of your psyche, such as your inner critic, your wounded child, or your wise elder. By giving voice and form to these inner characters, you can begin to understand their needs, fears, and gifts, and to develop a more integrated and harmonious sense of self.

As you broaden your awareness of your inner world, it is equally important to expand your understanding of the universe and your place within it. This involves cultivating a sense of awe, wonder, and reverence for the mystery and complexity of existence. It means recognizing that you are not separate from the cosmos, but rather an integral part of an interconnected web of life and consciousness.

One way to deepen your connection with the universe is through the practice of contemplation and communion with nature. By spending time in wild and beautiful places, and by attuning yourself to the rhythms and cycles of the natural world, you can begin to experience a profound sense of belonging and unity with all of life. You might engage in practices such as forest bathing, where you immerse yourself in the healing presence of trees and plants, or stargazing, where you allow yourself to be humbled and inspired by the vastness of the night sky.

Another pathway for expanding your awareness of the universe is through the study of science, philosophy, and spirituality. By exposing yourself to diverse perspectives and paradigms, and by grappling with the big questions of existence, you can begin to stretch your mind and heart beyond the confines of your familiar beliefs and assumptions. You might explore fields such as quantum physics, neuroscience, or comparative religion, allowing yourself to be challenged and enriched by the insights and discoveries of great thinkers and practitioners throughout history.

Ultimately, the process of broadening your awareness of inner self, thought patterns, and the universe is a journey of integration and wholeness. It involves recognizing that your individual consciousness is a microcosm of the greater macrocosm, and that by exploring the depths of your own being, you are simultaneously unfolding the mysteries of the cosmos. As you expand your awareness in all directions, you begin to experience a profound sense of interconnectedness, meaning, and purpose.

This journey of integration is not always easy, as it requires you to confront the shadows and limitations within yourself and the world around you. Yet, as you navigate this path with courage, compassion, and curiosity, you open yourself to a reality that is infinitely more rich, dynamic, and alive than you could have ever imagined. You begin to recognize that every aspect of your being, from your deepest wounds to your highest aspirations, is a sacred part of the grand tapestry of existence, and that by embracing the fullness of your humanity, you are participating in the ongoing evolution of consciousness itself.

As you continue to broaden your awareness and deepen your engagement with the game of life, trust that you are exactly where you need to be, and that every experience, whether joyful or challenging, is an opportunity for growth, healing, and transformation. Embrace the journey with an open heart and a curious mind, knowing that the universe is conspiring in your favor, and that your unique path of awakening is an essential part of the collective unfolding of our world. May your expanding consciousness be a beacon of light and inspiration for all those you encounter, and may your presence on this Earth be a blessing for generations to come.

Transitioning from passive player to active participant in the game of life is a transformative shift that occurs as you expand your consciousness and deepen your understanding of your creative potential. It involves moving beyond the illusion of being a victim of circumstance, and instead embracing your role as a powerful co-creator of your reality. This shift is not always easy, as it requires you to take responsibility for your experiences, and to confront the ways in which you may have been limiting yourself through unconscious patterns of thought and behavior.

One of the key aspects of becoming an active participant is developing a strong sense of agency and self-efficacy. This means believing in your ability to influence your life circumstances, and trusting in your capacity to navigate challenges and opportunities with skill and resilience. It involves cultivating a proactive mindset, where you focus your energy on the things you can control, rather than getting caught up in the drama and chaos of external events.

To strengthen your sense of agency, you might engage in practices such as goal-setting and visualization. By clarifying your intentions and desires, and by regularly imagining yourself achieving your objectives, you can begin to align your thoughts, emotions, and actions with your highest aspirations. You might also explore techniques such as affirmations and self-hypnosis, which can help you to rewire your subconscious mind and cultivate a more empowered and confident sense of self.

Another key aspect of becoming an active participant is learning to listen to and trust your intuition. Your intuition is the voice of your higher self, the part of you that is connected to the wisdom and intelligence of the universe. By developing a strong relationship with your intuition, you can begin to access a deeper level of guidance and insight, and to make choices that are aligned with your authentic path and purpose.

To cultivate your intuition, you might explore practices such as meditation, journaling, or creative expression. By quieting your mind and tuning into your inner world, you can begin to discern the subtle whispers of your intuitive knowing, and to distinguish them from the noise and chatter of your ego and conditioning. You might also seek out opportunities to explore your dreams, synchronicities, and other forms of symbolic communication, as these can often provide valuable clues and messages from your higher self.

As you transition from passive player to active participant, you may also find it helpful to cultivate a spirit of experimentation and play. Rather than approaching life with a rigid or serious mindset, allow yourself to engage with the world with a sense of curiosity, openness, and wonder. Be willing to take risks, to try new things, and to learn from your mistakes and failures. Embrace the idea that life is a grand adventure, and that every experience, whether joyful or challenging, is an opportunity for growth and discovery.

One way to cultivate a spirit of play is to engage in activities that bring you joy and fulfillment, without attachment to specific outcomes or results. This might involve pursuing hobbies or interests that allow you to express your creativity, connect with others, or explore new aspects of yourself. It might also involve volunteering or contributing to causes that align with your values and passions, as a way of making a positive impact on the world around you.

As you become a more active participant in the game of life, you may also find it valuable to seek out communities of like-minded individuals who share your values and aspirations. By surrounding yourself with people who support and inspire you, you can accelerate your growth and expand your perspective in ways that may not be possible on your own. You might join a spiritual or personal development group, attend workshops or retreats, or seek out mentors or coaches who can provide guidance and encouragement on your path.

Ultimately, the transition from passive player to active participant is a journey of empowerment and self-realization. It involves recognizing that you are not a helpless pawn in the game of life, but rather a powerful creator with the ability to shape your reality through your thoughts, beliefs, and actions. As you step into this role with courage and conviction, you begin to experience a profound sense of freedom, purpose, and possibility.

This is not to say that the journey of active participation is always easy or straightforward. There will be times when you face challenges, setbacks, and obstacles that test your resolve and resilience. There will be moments when you feel lost, confused, or overwhelmed by the complexity of the game. Yet, it is precisely in these moments that your commitment to growth and self-discovery will be most essential.

When you encounter difficulties on your path, remember to approach them with a spirit of curiosity and compassion. Rather than getting caught up in self-judgment or blame, ask yourself what lessons and opportunities for growth are hidden within the challenge. Trust that every experience, no matter how painful or difficult, is ultimately serving your highest evolution and unfolding.

As you continue to embrace your role as an active participant in the game of life, you may find that your definition of success and fulfillment begins to shift. Rather than chasing after external markers of achievement or validation, you may discover a deeper sense of meaning and purpose that arises from living in alignment with your authentic self and contributing to the greater good of all. You may find that your greatest joy and satisfaction comes from expressing your unique gifts and talents in service of something larger than yourself.

Ultimately, the journey of becoming an active participant is a lifelong process of learning, growth, and self-discovery. It requires a willingness to embrace change, to take risks, and to face your fears and limitations with honesty and courage. Yet, as you navigate this path with an open heart and a curious mind, you open yourself to a reality that is infinitely more rich, dynamic, and fulfilling than you could have ever imagined.

So, as you continue to expand your consciousness and deepen your engagement with the game of life, remember that you are never alone on this journey. You are part of a vast web of consciousness that is constantly evolving and unfolding, and your unique path of awakening is an essential thread in the tapestry of existence. Trust in the wisdom and intelligence of the universe, and know that every step you take, no matter how small or uncertain, is a vital part of the grand adventure of life.

If you feel inspired by the ideas and practices explored in this chapter and wish to dive deeper into the process of expanding your consciousness, I invite you to check out the Wisdom Academy. This comprehensive online course is designed to provide you with a structured, immersive, and transformative learning experience, empowering you with the tools, insights, and support you need to navigate the game of life with greater wisdom, clarity, and purpose. Through rich teachings, practices, and reflections, the Wisdom Academy will guide you in cultivating a profound understanding of yourself, the universe, and your place within it, helping you to step forth as an active co-creator of your reality and a beacon of light in the world.

Click **here** or **Scan the QR code below** to Learn More.

WISDOM
ACADEMY

Chapter Five

Listening to Your Guidance System

Your feelings, gut, and intuition as a compass, a powerful inner guidance system that navigates you through the complex terrain of life. As we journey through the twists and turns of our individual paths, we are not left alone to fumble in the dark. Within each of us lies a profound source of wisdom, an internal compass that points us towards our true north, aligning us with our deepest values, desires, and purpose.

Learning to attune ourselves to this inner guidance is a crucial skill in the art of conscious living. In a world filled with endless distractions, external pressures, and conflicting voices, it is all too easy to become disconnected from our authentic truth. We may find ourselves swayed by the opinions of others, chasing after goals that leave us feeling hollow, or making choices that are out of alignment with our core essence.

Yet, when we cultivate a deep and trusting relationship with our feelings, gut instincts, and intuitive promptings, we gain access to a powerful ally in the unfolding of our lives. Our emotions, far from being irrational or unreliable, are actually sophisticated messengers, conveying vital information about our needs, boundaries, and true desires. By learning to honor and listen to our feelings, we develop a greater capacity for self-awareness, authenticity, and self-care.

One of the key aspects of attuning to our emotional guidance system is developing a language of sensation and body awareness. This involves learning to recognize and name the subtle physical cues that accompany our various emotional states. For example, we may notice that anxiety manifests as a tightness in our chest, while joy radiates as a warm expansiveness in our heart center. By bringing mindful attention to these bodily sensations, we can gain valuable insights into our inner landscape, using our felt experience as a compass to navigate life's challenges and opportunities.

Another crucial component of our inner guidance system is our intuition, that still, small voice within that speaks to us through flashes of insight, gut feelings, and synchronistic experiences. Intuition is the language of our subconscious mind, a direct line to the vast reservoir of wisdom and creativity that lies beneath the surface of our everyday awareness. By learning to trust and act upon our intuitive promptings, we open ourselves to a world of possibility and divine guidance.

Cultivating a strong connection to our intuition requires a willingness to quiet the noise of our rational mind and create space for the whispers of our inner knowing to emerge. This can involve practices such as meditation, journaling, or spending time in nature, allowing ourselves to slip into a state of receptive awareness. As we learn to discern the voice of our intuition from the chatter of our ego or the influence of external expectations, we gain a powerful tool for making aligned decisions and navigating life's uncertainties with grace and confidence.

Listening to our inner guidance system also involves developing a deep sense of trust in the intelligence of the universe and the inherent rightness of our own path. This can be a challenging practice, especially when our intuitive promptings seem to defy logic or lead us in directions that feel risky or unfamiliar. Yet, by cultivating a sense of faith and surrendering to the greater unfolding of our lives, we open ourselves to the magic and synchronicity that arise when we are in flow with our true purpose.

One powerful way to strengthen our connection to our inner guidance is to regularly engage in practices of self-reflection and inquiry. This can involve setting aside time each day to tune into our feelings and intuitive impressions, asking ourselves questions such as: "What is my heart calling me to do in this moment? What feels most aligned with my deepest values and aspirations? What messages are my emotions and body sensations conveying to me?"

By bringing curiosity and compassion to our inner experience, we create a safe space for our authentic wisdom to emerge. We learn to distinguish between the voice of our true self and the internalized messages of fear, limitation, or external conditioning. As we practice honoring and acting upon our inner guidance, we begin to cultivate a deep sense of self-trust and inner authority, becoming the sovereign creators of our own reality.

Of course, learning to listen to our inner guidance system is not always a linear or easy process. There may be times when our emotions feel overwhelming, our intuition seems unclear, or our gut instincts lead us in challenging directions. In these moments, it is important to remember that our inner wisdom is not separate from the greater intelligence of the universe. By surrendering our doubts and fears to a higher power, and trusting in the inherent rightness of our unfolding journey, we can find the courage and clarity to keep moving forward.

Ultimately, attuning to our feelings, gut, and intuition is a lifelong practice, one that requires patience, self-compassion, and a willingness to embrace the full spectrum of our human experience. As we learn to honor and trust our inner guidance system, we become more authentic, empowered, and aligned with our true purpose. We navigate life's challenges and opportunities with greater ease and grace, knowing that we are always being guided towards our highest good.

By cultivating a deep and loving relationship with our inner compass, we open ourselves to a world of magic, synchronicity, and limitless possibility. We become co-creators with the divine, aligning our unique gifts and aspirations with the greater unfolding of the cosmos. As we learn to trust and follow the wisdom within, we not only transform our own lives but also contribute to the healing and awakening of the entire planet.

So let us each take a moment to pause, to breathe deeply, and to tune into the still, small voice within. Let us ask ourselves, with open hearts and curious minds: "What is my inner guidance system calling me to do, to be, to create in this precious moment?" And let us have the courage and faith to listen, to trust, and to act upon the wisdom that emerges, knowing that every step we take is a sacred dance with the divine, weaving the tapestry of our lives into the greater masterpiece of existence.

Resonance as a key to alignment with your true path, a vibrational language that guides you towards your authentic expression and purpose. Just as a tuning fork vibrates in harmony with its matching frequency, we too possess an inner resonance, a unique energetic signature that reflects our deepest truths, values, and aspirations. When we learn to attune ourselves to this internal resonance, we tap into a powerful compass that aligns us with our true path, guiding us towards experiences, relationships, and opportunities that are in harmony with our highest potential.

At its core, resonance is a feeling of deep alignment, a sense of "rightness" that emanates from the very center of our being. It is a visceral knowing that transcends the limitations of the rational mind, speaking to us through the language of the heart and the wisdom of the body. When we encounter people, places, or ideas that resonate with our true essence, we feel a sense of expansion, inspiration, and joy – as if our entire being is saying "yes" to the experience.

Cultivating a deep attunement to our inner resonance is a crucial skill in navigating the complex landscape of life. In a world filled with countless paths and possibilities, it is all too easy to become distracted by external influences, societal expectations, or the opinions of others. We may find ourselves pursuing goals or relationships that feel hollow or misaligned, simply because we have lost touch with our own inner truth.

By learning to trust and follow our resonance, we begin to chart a course that is uniquely our own, one that honors our authentic desires, talents, and values. This requires a willingness to listen deeply to ourselves, to pay attention to the subtle cues and messages that arise from within. It involves cultivating a relationship of trust and respect with our inner guidance system, recognizing that our feelings and intuitions are powerful allies in the unfolding of our lives.

One of the key ways to strengthen our connection to our inner resonance is through practices of self-discovery and self-reflection. This can involve exploring our passions and interests, clarifying our values and beliefs, and investigating the unique gifts and talents that we bring to the world. By taking the time to know ourselves on a deep level – our strengths, challenges, dreams, and fears – we create a solid foundation from which to navigate life's choices and opportunities.

Another powerful tool for aligning with our resonance is the practice of embodiment – learning to fully inhabit and trust the wisdom of our physical being. Our bodies are exquisitely attuned to the vibrational language of the universe, constantly providing us with feedback and guidance through sensations, emotions, and intuitive promptings. By cultivating a deep and loving relationship with our body, we gain access to a powerful source of inner knowing, one that can guide us towards experiences and choices that are truly nourishing and fulfilling.

Aligning with our resonance also involves developing a willingness to let go of that which no longer serves us. This can include relationships, beliefs, or patterns of behavior that feel draining, limiting, or misaligned with our authentic truth. While it may be challenging to release these old attachments, doing so creates space for new possibilities to emerge, allowing us to step more fully into our true path and purpose.

As we learn to trust and follow our inner resonance, we may find ourselves drawn to explore new avenues of expression, creativity, and service. We may feel called to take bold risks, to step outside our comfort zone, and to pursue dreams that once seemed impossible. By staying true to our inner compass, we become co-creators with the universe, aligning our unique gifts and passions with the greater unfolding of the cosmos.

Of course, the journey of resonance is not always a straightforward or easy path. There may be times when our inner guidance feels unclear, when we encounter obstacles or challenges that test our faith and resolve. In these moments, it is important to remember that our resonance is not a static or fixed destination, but rather a dynamic and evolving process of growth and self-discovery.

By cultivating a spirit of curiosity, compassion, and self-trust, we can navigate the ups and downs of our journey with grace and resilience. We learn to embrace the full spectrum of our human experience – the joys and sorrows, the triumphs and failures – recognizing that every moment is an opportunity to deepen our alignment with our true path and purpose.

Ultimately, attuning to our inner resonance is a lifelong practice, one that requires patience, commitment, and a willingness to listen to the whispers of our soul. As we learn to honor and trust the unique frequency of our being, we become powerful agents of transformation, not only for ourselves but for the world around us. We inspire others through our authenticity and integrity, demonstrating the incredible beauty and potential that arises when we dare to live in alignment with our deepest truth.

So let us each take a moment to pause, to quiet the noise of the external world, and to tune into the vibrant resonance that emanates from within. Let us ask ourselves, with open hearts and curious minds: "What does my soul long to express, to create, to become in this precious lifetime?" And let us have the courage and faith to follow that resonance, step by step, knowing that every choice we make in alignment with our true path is a sacred gift to ourselves and to the greater tapestry of existence.

May we all find the strength and wisdom to embrace the journey of resonance, to trust in the unfolding of our own unique destiny, and to contribute our gifts and talents to the healing and awakening of our world. For when we each shine our light in full alignment with our authentic truth, we create a radiant web of inspiration and possibility, illuminating the path for all those who follow in our footsteps.

Discerning between ego-driven desires and true resonance is a crucial skill in navigating the path of authentic alignment and purpose. In the complex landscape of our inner world, there are many voices that vie for our attention – the demands of our ego, the expectations of others, and the deep, often subtle whispers of our soul. Learning to distinguish between these different impulses is a key aspect of cultivating a life that is truly fulfilling and meaningful.

At its core, the ego is the part of our psyche that is concerned with survival, status, and self-preservation. It is the voice that tells us we need to be successful, admired, and in control, often at the expense of our deeper values and desires. While the ego plays an important role in helping us navigate the practical demands of life, it can also lead us astray, convincing us to pursue goals and relationships that are ultimately unfulfilling or even harmful.

In contrast, true resonance arises from a place of deep soul alignment – a sense of purpose, meaning, and connection that goes beyond the fleeting satisfaction of the ego. When we are in touch with our true resonance, we feel a sense of expansion, inspiration, and joy that emanates from the very core of our being. We are drawn to experiences, people, and opportunities that feel deeply nourishing and fulfilling, even if they don't always conform to society's definitions of success or happiness.

One of the key ways to discern between ego-driven desires and true resonance is to cultivate a practice of self-inquiry and reflection. This involves taking the time to sit with ourselves, to listen deeply to the stirrings of our heart and soul, and to ask honest questions about our motivations and intentions. We might ask ourselves: "What is the deeper purpose behind this desire? Is it coming from a place of fear, scarcity, or the need for external validation? Or is it arising from a place of love, abundance, and authentic self-expression?"

Another powerful tool for discernment is the practice of body awareness and embodiment. Our physical being is a highly attuned instrument, constantly providing us with feedback and guidance through sensations, emotions, and intuitive promptings. When we are in alignment with our true resonance, we often feel a sense of open-ness, ease, and vitality in our body. In contrast, when we are pursuing ego-driven desires, we may experience feelings of contraction, tension, or depletion – as if our body is sending us a clear signal that something is out of alignment.

Discerning between ego and resonance also involves developing a willingness to let go of attachments and expectations. The ego often clings tightly to specific outcomes or ideas of how things "should" be, leading us to feel frustrated, anxious, or disappointed when life doesn't conform to our plans. In contrast, true resonance involves a deep trust in the unfolding of our path, a willingness to surrender to the mystery and magic of life, even when it takes us in unexpected directions.

As we learn to navigate the complex landscape of our desires, it is important to approach the process with compassion and self-love. The journey of discernment is not about judging or rejecting parts of ourselves, but rather about bringing a curious and loving attention to all aspects of our being. By creating a safe and nurturing space for self-exploration, we can begin to unravel the layers of conditioning and fear that may be obscuring our true resonance, gradually aligning ourselves with a deeper sense of purpose and authenticity.

One powerful practice for cultivating discernment is the art of con-templation and meditation. By taking time each day to quiet the mind and tune into the deeper currents of our being, we create space for our true resonance to emerge. We might practice sitting in silence, focusing on the breath or a sacred word, and simply observing the thoughts, feelings, and sensations that arise. As we become more skilled in wit-nessing our inner experience with nonjudgmental awareness, we begin to develop a clearer sense of the different voices and impulses that are shaping our choices and actions.

Another valuable tool for discernment is the practice of journaling and self-reflection. By taking time to write down our thoughts, feelings, and experiences, we create a mirror for ourselves, revealing patterns and insights that may be difficult to see in the moment. We can use our journal as a space for honest inquiry, exploring questions such as: "What are my deepest values and priorities? What brings me true joy and fulfillment? What are the fears and beliefs that may be holding me back from my authentic path?"

As we continue to practice discernment, we may find that our true resonance leads us in surprising or unconventional directions. We may feel called to pursue a creative passion, to start a new business, or to embark on a spiritual journey that challenges our previous assumptions and beliefs. While these choices may feel risky or uncertain at times, they are also an opportunity to align ourselves with a deeper sense of meaning and purpose, to contribute our unique gifts and talents to the world in a way that truly lights us up.

Ultimately, the journey of discerning between ego-driven desires and true resonance is a lifelong practice, one that requires patience, self-compassion, and a willingness to embrace the unknown. As we learn to listen deeply to the whispers of our soul, to trust in the unfolding of our own unique path, we become powerful agents of transformation – not only for ourselves but for all those whose lives we touch.

So let us each take a moment to pause, to breathe deeply, and to attune ourselves to the deeper currents of our being. Let us ask ourselves, with open hearts and curious minds: "What is my soul's deepest desire? What is the truth that wants to be expressed through me in this precious lifetime?" And let us have the courage and faith to follow that resonance, step by step, knowing that every choice we make in alignment with our authentic truth is a sacred gift to ourselves and to the world.

May we all find the clarity and wisdom to navigate the complex landscape of our desires, to discern between the voices of ego and the whispers of our soul. And may we each have the strength and resilience to pursue our true resonance, even in the face of fear or uncertainty – trusting that every step we take in alignment with our deepest truth is a powerful contribution to the healing and awakening of our world.

Chapter Six

The Mirror of the Subconscious

The subconscious mind's impartiality and lack of intentionality is a fundamental principle that underlies the process of personal transformation and growth. Unlike the conscious mind, which is often driven by specific goals, judgments, and agendas, the subconscious mind is a neutral and objective storehouse of all the experiences, beliefs, and conditioning that you have accumulated over the course of your life.

This impartiality means that the subconscious mind does not filter or discriminate between positive and negative input, but rather absorbs and reflects back to you whatever information and experiences you expose it to, whether consciously or unconsciously. Just as a mirror simply reflects the image that stands before it, without any agenda or bias, so too does the subconscious mind reflect back to you the sum total of your mental and emotional programming.

The impact of social conditioning and personal experiences on the subconscious cannot be overstated. From the moment you are born, you are immersed in a complex web of cultural, familial, and societal influences that shape your beliefs, values, and perceptions in profound ways. The messages you receive from your parents, teachers, peers, and the media all contribute to the formation of your subconscious mind, creating a unique lens through which you interpret and navigate the world.

Personal experiences, too, play a powerful role in shaping the subconscious mind. The events and circumstances of your life, particularly those that occur during your early years, can leave a deep and lasting imprint on your psyche, influencing your patterns of thought, emotion, and behavior in often unconscious ways. Traumatic experiences, for example, can create subconscious patterns of fear, anxiety, or mistrust that persist long after the original event has passed, coloring your perceptions and reactions in subtle but significant ways.

It's important to recognize that not all of the conditioning and experiences that shape your subconscious mind are positive or empowering. In fact, many of the beliefs and patterns that you absorb from your environment may be limiting, self-sabotaging, or even harmful. The responsibility of filtering unhealthy thoughts, therefore, falls upon your conscious mind – the part of you that has the ability to observe, question, and choose which thoughts and beliefs to embrace and which to release.

This process of conscious filtration begins with self-awareness – the willingness to honestly and objectively observe your own patterns of thought and behavior, without judgment or self-criticism. By cultivating a practice of mindfulness and self-reflection, you can begin to identify the subconscious beliefs and assumptions that are shaping your experience of reality, and to question their validity and usefulness in your current context.

When you notice a thought or belief that feels limiting, negative, or disempowering, you have the power to consciously choose a different perspective. This might involve challenging the thought with evidence to the contrary, reframing it in a more positive or expansive light, or simply acknowledging it with compassion and then releasing it, rather than allowing it to take root in your subconscious mind.

The practice of filtering unhealthy thoughts is an ongoing process, one that requires patience, persistence, and self-compassion. It's important to remember that your subconscious mind has been shaped by a lifetime of conditioning and experiences, and it may take time and repetition to reprogram deeply ingrained patterns of belief and behavior. Be gentle with yourself as you navigate this process, celebrating your successes and learning from your challenges along the way.

As you continue to take responsibility for the thoughts and beliefs that you allow into your subconscious mind, you may find that your experience of reality begins to shift in profound ways. By consciously choosing to focus your attention on that which is positive, empowering, and aligned with your highest truth, you begin to reshape your subconscious mind, attracting experiences and opportunities that reflect your deepest desires and aspirations.

Ultimately, the subconscious mind is a powerful tool for personal transformation and growth, but it is up to you to harness its potential and direct its energy in service of your highest good. By understanding the impartiality and malleability of the subconscious mind, and by taking responsibility for the quality and content of your mental and emotional input, you become the master of your own reality, shaping your life and the world around you in beautiful and transformative ways.

So embrace the power and potential of your subconscious mind, and commit to the ongoing practice of self-awareness, self-reflection, and conscious choice. Trust in your own innate wisdom and resilience, and know that every thought you choose to embrace is a step towards the life you were born to live. You are the creator of your own reality, and the subconscious mind is your faithful partner in the journey of growth and awakening. Let your light shine, and trust that all is unfolding exactly as it is meant to, in perfect time and perfect way.

Chapter Seven

Harnessing the Power of Repetition

Actively reprogramming subconscious beliefs through repetition is a transformative practice that empowers you to reshape your inner landscape and manifest your deepest desires and aspirations. By consistently exposing your mind to positive, empowering thoughts and experiences, you gradually rewire your neural pathways, creating new patterns of belief and behavior that align with your highest potential and purpose.

Repetition is a powerful tool for change because it works in harmony with the natural plasticity of your brain. Every time you repeat a thought, affirmation, or action, you strengthen the corresponding neural connections, making it easier and more automatic to access those patterns in the future. Over time, with consistent practice, these new patterns become deeply ingrained in your subconscious mind, shaping your perceptions, emotions, and behaviors in profound ways.

To effectively harness the power of repetition, it's important to approach the process with intention, consistency, and self-compassion. Begin by clarifying your desired beliefs and outcomes, and create a simple, affirmative statement or visualization that encapsulates the essence of what you wish to manifest. For example, if you wish to cultivate greater self-love and confidence, you might repeat a statement such as "I am worthy, capable, and deeply loved," or visualize yourself moving through the world with ease and assurance.

The importance of feeling the desired state cannot be overstated when it comes to reprogramming your subconscious mind. Your emotions are the language of your inner being, and when you infuse your repetitions with positive feeling states, you amplify their power and effectiveness. As you repeat your affirmations or visualizations, take a moment to connect with the energy and emotion of your desired state, allowing yourself to fully embody the experience as if it were already your present reality.

You might imagine the warmth and expansiveness of self-love filling your body, or the calm, centered confidence that comes from trusting in your own abilities and worth. The more vividly and emotionally you engage with your desired state, the more powerfully it will imprint upon your subconscious mind, attracting corresponding experiences and opportunities into your life.

As you continue to practice repetition, it's important to align your actions, behavior, and words with your newfound beliefs. Consistency is key when it comes to reprogramming your subconscious mind, and every choice you make either reinforces or undermines your desired reality. Begin to notice the small ways in which you can embody your new beliefs in your daily life, whether that be through speaking kindly to yourself, setting healthy boundaries, or taking bold action towards your goals.

Remember that change is a gradual process, and it's normal to encounter resistance or setbacks along the way. Be gentle and patient with yourself, celebrating your progress and learning from your challenges as you go. Surround yourself with supportive influences and resources that reflect your desired state, and continue to feed your mind with positive, uplifting input on a regular basis.

As you harness the power of repetition and align your actions with your beliefs, you may find that your external reality begins to shift in miraculous and unexpected ways. New opportunities, relationships, and experiences that align with your highest good will naturally flow into your life, as you become a vibrational match for the reality you desire. Trust in the process and keep your focus on the present moment, knowing that every repetition is a powerful act of creation and manifestation.

Ultimately, the practice of reprogramming your subconscious mind through repetition is a sacred act of self-love and self-care. By choosing to focus your mind and energy on that which uplifts and inspires you, you reclaim your power as the creator of your own reality, shaping your life and the world around you in beautiful and transformative ways. As you continue on this path of growth and awakening, know that you are supported by the infinite wisdom and love of the universe, and that your unique journey is unfolding exactly as it is meant to.

So embrace the power of repetition with open arms, and trust in your own innate ability to manifest the life of your dreams. Stay committed to your practice, both internally and externally, and watch as your reality blossoms into a radiant expression of your deepest truth and potential. You are a powerful creator, a divine being in human form, and the universe is conspiring in your favor, now and always. Let your light shine, and know that every repetition is a step towards the life you were born to live.

Chapter Eight

You Are the Universe

Speaking to the universe as speaking to your higher self is a profound realization that can transform your entire perspective on life. As you come to understand the deep interconnectedness between your individual consciousness and the greater cosmic intelligence, you begin to recognize that you are not separate from the universe, but rather an integral part of its ever-unfolding expression.

When you speak to the universe, you are essentially engaging in a dialogue with your own deepest wisdom and potential. You are tapping into the infinite well of creativity, resilience, and love that resides within you, and aligning yourself with the greater flow of life itself. By cultivating a relationship of trust and openness with the universe, you open yourself up to a world of limitless possibility and support, knowing that you are always guided and protected by a benevolent force greater than yourself.

Taking control and aligning your consciousness with positivity is a powerful way to harness the creative potential of the universe and manifest your deepest desires and aspirations. By choosing to focus your attention on the good, the beautiful, and the true, you begin to shift your vibrational frequency and attract more of those qualities into your life. You become a magnet for positive experiences, relationships, and opportunities, and radiate a sense of joy, gratitude, and abundance wherever you go.

Of course, aligning your consciousness with positivity is not always easy, particularly in the face of life's challenges and obstacles. There may be times when you feel overwhelmed, discouraged, or stuck, and it can be tempting to slip back into old patterns of negative thinking or self-doubt. However, by developing a consistent practice of mindfulness, affirmation, and self-care, you can train your mind to default to a state of positivity and resilience, even in the midst of difficulty.

One powerful way to align your consciousness with positivity is to cultivate a daily practice of gratitude and appreciation. By taking time each day to focus on the blessings and miracles in your life, no matter how small, you begin to shift your perception and attract more of those experiences to you. You might keep a gratitude journal, share your appreciation with others, or simply take a few moments each day to silently acknowledge the goodness and beauty that surrounds you.

Another key aspect of aligning your consciousness with positivity is to surround yourself with uplifting and inspiring influences, whether that be through the people you associate with, the media you consume, or the environments you immerse yourself in. By choosing to fill your mind and heart with messages of hope, beauty, and possibility, you create a powerful force field of positive energy that radiates out into the world around you, influencing and uplifting others in turn.

As you deepen your practice of aligning your consciousness with positivity, you may find that your reality begins to shift in miraculous and unexpected ways. You may encounter new opportunities, relationships, and experiences that reflect your highest values and aspirations, and feel a profound sense of purpose and fulfillment in all that you do. You begin to recognize that your reality is truly your canvas, and that you are the artist with the power to create a masterpiece of your own design.

Your reality as your canvas and you as the artist is a profound truth that empowers you to take full responsibility for the life you are creating, moment by moment. When you recognize that your thoughts, beliefs, and actions are the brushstrokes that shape your experience of reality, you begin to wield your creative power with greater intention and skill. You become the master of your own destiny, consciously choosing the colors, textures, and composition of your life's greatest work of art.

Of course, creating a masterpiece of your life is not always a straightforward or easy process. There may be times when you feel uninspired, blocked, or frustrated, or when external circumstances seem to be conspiring against your vision. However, by staying connected to your own inner wisdom and trusting in the greater unfolding of the universe, you can navigate these challenges with grace and resilience, knowing that every experience is an opportunity for growth and learning.

One helpful way to approach your reality as your canvas is to cultivate a sense of playfulness, experimentation, and curiosity in all that you do. Rather than getting attached to specific outcomes or expectations, allow yourself to explore new possibilities and ideas, trusting that the universe will guide you towards your highest good. Be willing to take risks, to step outside your comfort zone, and to embrace the unknown, knowing that every choice you make is a stroke of paint on the canvas of your life.

Another key aspect of being the artist of your reality is to cultivate a deep sense of self-love, self-acceptance, and self-compassion. Just as a great artist pours their heart and soul into their work, infusing it with their unique essence and vision, so too must you learn to love and accept yourself fully, embracing your own quirks, flaws, and imperfections as part of the beautiful tapestry of your being. By treating yourself with kindness, understanding, and respect, you create a foundation of inner peace and resilience that allows you to weather any storm and create from a place of authentic power.

As you continue to align your consciousness with positivity and embrace your role as the artist of your reality, you may find that your life begins to unfold in ways that are truly extraordinary and deeply fulfilling. You may discover new talents, passions, and callings that light you up from the inside out, and feel a profound sense of connection and purpose in all that you do. By staying true to your own unique vision and trusting in the wisdom of the universe, you can create a life that is a true work of art, filled with beauty, meaning, and endless possibility.

If you have found value and inspiration in the ideas and practices shared in this book, I invite you to take a moment to leave a review on your preferred platform, whether that be Amazon, Goodreads, or elsewhere. Your honest feedback and reflection not only helps to spread the message of this book to a wider audience, but also serves as a powerful act of co-creation, helping to shape the collective consciousness and evolution of humanity.

By sharing your own experiences, insights, and transformations, you become a beacon of light and hope for others who may be struggling or seeking guidance on their own path of growth and awakening. Your words have the power to touch hearts, open minds, and inspire others to embark on their own journey of self-discovery and transformation, creating a ripple effect of positive change that extends far beyond your own individual life.

Moreover, by taking the time to leave a review, you help to amplify the visibility and reach of this book, making it more likely to show up for other readers who may be in need of its message and guidance. In a world that is increasingly saturated with information and noise, your review serves as a powerful signal of resonance and alignment, helping to connect this book with its ideal audience and maximizing its potential for impact and transformation.

So if you feel called to do so, I invite you to take a few moments to reflect on your own journey with this book, and to share your thoughts and experiences with others. Whether your review is long or short, positive or constructively critical, know that your voice matters and that your contribution is deeply appreciated. Together, we can create a world of greater understanding, compassion, and possibility, one book and one review at a time.

If you're ready to take the next step on your journey of self-discovery and alignment with the universe, I encourage you to explore the Wisdom Academy. This transformative online course is designed to support you in integrating the insights and practices from this book into your daily life, providing you with the tools, guidance, and community you need to accelerate your growth and manifest your deepest desires. With in-depth teachings, guided meditations, live Q&A sessions, and a supportive community of like-minded individuals, the Wisdom Academy is the perfect resource to empower you on your path. Join us today and unlock your full potential as a conscious creator.

Scan the QR code below to Learn More

Thank you for being a part of this journey, and for your willingness to co-create a brighter, more beautiful future for us all. May your own path be filled with endless growth, discovery, and joy, and may you always remember the incredible power and potential that resides within you. You are the universe, and the universe is speaking through you. Let your light shine, and trust that all is unfolding in perfect time and perfect way.

www.ingramcontent.com/pod-product-compliance
Lightning Source LLC
Chambersburg PA
CBHW072036150726
47999CB00002B/934